Digital Gold Rush

Navigating the Future of Finance

with Cryptocurrency and AI

Bruce Goldwell

Disclaimer

Please note that the content provided in this book is for educational and informational purposes only. The author of this book is not a licensed investment counselor, financial advisor, or legal expert. The information presented herein is not intended to serve as financial, investment, legal, or tax advice, nor should it be used as the basis for making investment decisions.

The financial market, particularly in areas concerning cryptocurrencies and artificial intelligence (AI) in trading and investing, is highly volatile and subject to significant risks. While this book aims to furnish readers with a comprehensive understanding of the evolution of money, the emergence of cryptocurrency and blockchain technology, and the potential of AI in finance, it is crucial for readers to conduct their own thorough research and consider seeking advice from qualified professionals in the financial, legal, and tax fields before making any investment decisions.

The author and publisher have made every effort to ensure the accuracy of the information within this book at the time of publication. However, the financial landscape is constantly evolving, and the applicability or accuracy of the contents may change over time. The author and publisher disclaim any liability for any personal, business, or financial loss or damage that may result from the application of any information found in this book.

Investing in the financial market involves a significant degree of risk, including the loss of capital. Readers are advised to carefully consider their investment objectives, level of experience, and risk appetite before engaging in any trading or investment activities. The opportunities and strategies discussed in this book may not be suitable for all individuals or investors.

By proceeding beyond this disclaimer, readers acknowledge and agree that the use of any information derived from this book is at their own risk and discretion. The author and publisher shall not be held responsible for any outcomes or decisions made by readers based on the information provided herein.

Table of Contents

Revolutionizing Finance

"Wisdom isn't knowing everything-
it's knowing when to learn from
others."

Preface

Navigating the New Frontier of Finance

Welcome to a journey through the evolution of money—a narrative that not only charts the course of economic history but also sets the stage for understanding the revolutionary era we find ourselves in today. This book is an invitation to explore the intricate tapestry of financial innovation, from the earliest forms of barter to the digital currencies and blockchain technologies that are reshaping the global economy.

As we delve into the pages that follow, you will be guided through the milestones of monetary evolution, each chapter building upon the last, to provide a comprehensive understanding of how we arrived at the present moment. This exploration is not merely academic; it is a voyage that reveals the patterns of innovation and adaptation that have always been at the heart of financial progress. By understanding where we've come from, you'll be better equipped to grasp the transformative potential of where we're headed.

The advent of cryptocurrency and blockchain technology marks a pivotal chapter in this ongoing story of financial evolution. These digital innovations represent more than just new forms of currency; they are the harbingers of a decentralized financial future, offering unprecedented opportunities for growth, security, and inclusion. However, to fully appreciate their significance and potential, one must first understand the foundations upon which they are built.

This book aims to provide that understanding, laying the groundwork for an informed engagement with the digital financial landscape. Whether you are a seasoned investor, a curious observer, or somewhere in between, the insights contained herein will shed light on the complexities and opportunities of today's financial environment.

Moreover, as we stand on the cusp of another major leap forward—the integration of Artificial Intelligence (AI) in trading and investing—a new horizon of possibility emerges. The fusion of AI with cryptocurrency and blockchain technology opens up a realm of financial innovation that is as exciting as it is uncharted. The final sections of this book will introduce you to this burgeoning field, offering a glimpse into the AI-driven investment strategies that could redefine wealth generation in the digital age.

Included at the end of this book are resources for further exploration, as well as an introduction to a new income opportunity based on AI trading and investing. In an era where the pace of technological advancement continues to accelerate, the potential for financial empowerment and wealth creation is unprecedented. However, as with all opportunities, informed participation is key to success.

I encourage you to read through this book with an open mind and a critical eye, absorbing the lessons of the past as you contemplate the possibilities of the future. The evolution of money is an ongoing story, and you are part of its next chapter. The current explosion of AI and cryptocurrency offers a once-in-a-generation opportunity to capitalize on the cutting edge of financial technology. Let's embark on this journey together, with the knowledge that understanding our past is the first step toward seizing the opportunities of tomorrow.

Welcome to the new frontier of finance.

Before diving into the content of *Digital Gold Rush...*

the author wants to highlight crucial updates on the cryptocurrency landscape and why it's more important than ever for readers to act swiftly. Cryptocurrency is no longer just a trend—it's becoming an integral part of the global financial system, reshaping how we think about money, transactions, and wealth-building. The window of opportunity to secure your place in this digital revolution is rapidly closing as the market evolves and matures.

Here's why you need to act now:

Cryptocurrency is transforming industries from finance to technology, creating unprecedented opportunities for those who position themselves early. Major corporations, financial institutions, and even governments are investing in blockchain technology and digital currencies, recognizing their potential to redefine global commerce.

However, this growth also means that early movers stand to benefit the most. As mainstream adoption increases, the barriers to entry—both financial and technological—are rising. The days of getting in on the ground floor are limited. Acting quickly will give you a strategic advantage, enabling you to build a solid foundation in this emerging economy while others are still catching up.

Waiting too long to establish your position could mean missing out on life-changing opportunities. Those who understand the trends and take decisive action today will be the ones leading tomorrow's financial markets. The digital gold rush is happening now, and this is your chance to carve out your share before it's too late.

This book will guide you through the steps to make informed decisions and capitalize on the rapidly changing world of cryptocurrency—but first, you must be willing to seize the moment.

Comments by President Trump

....on Cryptocurrency

President Donald Trump has made several comments regarding cryptocurrency, particularly Bitcoin, during his presidency and beyond. His views have evolved over time, reflecting both skepticism and a recognition of the potential impact of digital currencies on the economy.

1. Initial Skepticism Towards Bitcoin

In July 2019, President Trump expressed skepticism about Bitcoin and other cryptocurrencies in a tweet where he stated that he was "not a fan" of Bitcoin. He raised concerns about the currency's volatility and its potential use for illegal activities. He emphasized that cryptocurrencies could undermine the U.S. dollar's status as the world's dominant currency, which is a significant concern for any sitting president given the importance of the dollar in global finance.

2. Emphasis on Regulation

Following his initial comments, Trump indicated that any cryptocurrency should be subject to regulation. He highlighted the need for regulatory frameworks to ensure consumer protection and prevent illicit activities associated with cryptocurrencies. This stance aligns with broader sentiments within government agencies like the Securities and Exchange Commission (SEC) and the Commodity Futures Trading Commission (CFTC), which have been working towards establishing clearer regulations for digital assets.

3. Support for Innovation in Blockchain Technology

Despite his critical remarks about Bitcoin specifically, Trump has acknowledged the potential benefits of blockchain technology—the underlying technology behind cryptocurrencies. In various speeches and interviews, he has pointed out that blockchain could revolutionize various sectors by enhancing transparency and efficiency in transactions.

4. Comments on Making America a Leader in Cryptocurrency

In recent discussions, Trump has suggested that America should aim to lead in cryptocurrency innovation rather than fall behind other nations like China, which has been actively developing its own digital currency initiatives. He has called for policies that would foster innovation while ensuring that American financial systems remain secure and competitive.

5. The Future of Cryptocurrency Under Trump's Influence

While Trump's administration did not implement specific policies aimed at promoting cryptocurrency directly, his comments have sparked discussions among lawmakers and industry leaders about how to position the U.S. as a leader in this emerging field. The dialogue around cryptocurrency continues to evolve as more stakeholders recognize its potential economic implications.

Conclusion

Trump's commentary on cryptocurrency reflects a careful balance between skepticism and recognition of its disruptive potential. His emphasis on regulation and consumer protection shows a cautious approach to this rapidly growing sector, while his acknowledgment of blockchain's benefits suggests an openness to technological advancement. As the U.S. navigates its role in the future of digital currencies, Trump's remarks have played a significant role in shaping the conversation, influencing how policymakers and industry leaders approach the complex world of cryptocurrency.

Latest Information on Ripple Gaining More Banks

Ripple, the company behind the XRP cryptocurrency, has been actively expanding its partnerships with banks and financial institutions globally. This growth is primarily driven by the increasing demand for efficient cross-border payment solutions that Ripple's technology offers. Here are some key points regarding Ripple's recent developments in gaining more banks:

1. **Partnership Expansion**: Ripple has successfully partnered with numerous financial institutions around the world. As of now, it has established connections with over 300 financial institutions, including major banks and payment providers. These partnerships enable these institutions to utilize Ripple's blockchain technology for faster and cheaper international transactions.

2. **On-Demand Liquidity (ODL)**: One of

Ripple's flagship products is its On-Demand Liquidity service, which allows financial institutions to source liquidity in real-time using XRP as a bridge currency. This service has gained traction among banks looking to reduce costs associated with pre-funding accounts in destination currencies.

3. **Regulatory Clarity**: The ongoing legal battle between Ripple and the U.S. Securities and Exchange Commission (SEC) has created uncertainty; however, recent rulings have provided some clarity regarding XRP's status as a digital asset rather than a security. This clarity is expected to encourage more banks to adopt Ripple's services without fear of regulatory repercussions.

4. **Technological Advancements**: Ripple continues to innovate its technology, making it appealing for banks seeking modern solutions for their payment systems. The introduction of features such as enhanced security protocols and improved transaction speeds positions Ripple favorably against traditional banking systems.

5. **Global Reach**: Ripple's focus on expanding into emerging markets has also been notable. By partnering with local

banks in regions such as Asia-Pacific and Latin America, Ripple aims to tap into new customer bases that require efficient remittance services.

6. **Industry Recognition**: As more banks adopt blockchain technology for their operations, Ripple has received recognition from industry analysts and experts as a leading provider of blockchain-based payment solutions, further solidifying its reputation in the financial sector.

In summary, through strategic partnerships, innovative products like ODL, regulatory advancements, technological improvements, global outreach efforts, and industry recognition,

Ripple is successfully gaining more banks as partners, enhancing its position within the financial ecosystem.

Ripple's recent expansion into the banking sector highlights the increasing adoption of blockchain technology to solve long-standing inefficiencies in cross-border payments. With over 300 financial institutions now using Ripple's blockchain, the company is revolutionizing international transactions by providing faster and more cost-effective solutions. The rise of Ripple's On-Demand Liquidity (ODL) service, which uses

XRP as a bridge currency, showcases how cryptocurrency can enhance liquidity management for banks.

The regulatory progress Ripple has made, particularly in the U.S., is also a significant factor in its growing influence. Although its legal battle with the SEC created uncertainty, recent rulings have clarified XRP's status, alleviating concerns about potential regulatory hurdles. This clarity, coupled with Ripple's constant technological innovations, has made the platform even more attractive for financial institutions.

Furthermore, Ripple's expansion into emerging markets, such as Asia-Pacific and Latin America, reflects its commitment to serving regions where remittance services are essential. By forming partnerships with local banks, Ripple continues to solidify its place in the global financial landscape.

In short, Ripple's strategy of combining innovative technology, regulatory engagement, and global partnerships is positioning it as a leader in the growing blockchain payment industry.

ChatGPT's Recommendation

There are several compelling reasons why XRP could be recommended to investors based on the information available:

1. Utility in Cross-Border Payments

XRP stands out because it serves a real-world purpose beyond being just a speculative asset. Ripple's On-Demand Liquidity (ODL) service uses XRP as a bridge currency, making international payments faster, cheaper, and more efficient. Traditional cross-border transactions can take days and involve high fees, while Ripple's technology allows near-instant transfers with lower costs. As global demand for faster and more efficient cross-border payment solutions grows, XRP could see increased utility and demand.

2. Partnerships with Financial Institutions

Ripple has established partnerships with over 300 financial institutions, including major banks and payment providers worldwide. These institutions are increasingly adopting Ripple's blockchain technology to improve their payment infrastructure. The broad use of Ripple's technology by large financial players positions XRP favorably as it is directly tied to this network.

3. Emerging Markets Expansion

Ripple's focus on emerging markets, particularly in regions like Asia-Pacific and Latin America, where remittances are vital, is another strong point. The need for fast, affordable cross-border payments is significant in these regions, and Ripple's technology offers a solution. As more institutions in these markets adopt Ripple's services, the demand for XRP is likely to grow, boosting its long-term value.

4. Regulatory Clarity

Ripple has been entangled in legal battles with the U.S. Securities and Exchange Commission (SEC), but recent developments have provided some clarity regarding the status of XRP as a digital asset rather than a security. This regulatory clarity removes some of the uncertainty surrounding XRP, making it a safer bet for investors looking for digital assets with clearer legal standing.

5. Technological Innovation

Ripple continues to enhance its technology, improving security, transaction speeds, and overall functionality. This ongoing innovation makes Ripple an attractive choice for institutions seeking cutting-edge solutions for payments, which, in turn, supports the value of XRP. As blockchain technology becomes more integral to the global financial system, XRP could benefit from being at the forefront of this transformation.

6. Position as a Bridge Currency

Ripple's vision for XRP as the "world's bridge currency" is significant. In a global economy with hundreds of different currencies, XRP's ability to act as a neutral intermediary between currencies during transactions could make it indispensable in international trade and finance.

7. Industry Recognition

Ripple has earned recognition from industry experts as a leading provider of blockchain-based payment solutions. Its strong reputation within the financial sector further legitimizes XRP's potential as a valuable asset.

Conclusion

Given its utility in global finance, widespread adoption by banks, emerging market focus, regulatory clarity, and continuous technological development, XRP presents a unique opportunity for investors. Its value is not solely based on market speculation but also on its practical use in solving real-world financial problems, making it a digital asset with substantial growth potential.

Author's Invitation

Based on President Trump's evolving views on

cryptocurrency and Ripple's ambitious growth, it's clear that the world of digital assets is moving toward a future of innovation and leadership. Ripple, with its On-Demand Liquidity service and global partnerships, is positioning itself as a critical player in the cross-border payment landscape, aiming to become the world's bridge capital for financial transactions.

With that in mind, the author personally invites you to join **Uphold**—one of the easiest and most cost-effective platforms for trading and managing your digital assets. Whether you're looking to explore Ripple (XRP) or other cryptocurrencies, Uphold offers a seamless experience that makes trading accessible for everyone.

Create your account today and experience the future of digital finance with Uphold: Sign Up Here >> https://bit.ly/CryptoAcct

I look forward to seeing you in this exciting new space!

Bruce Goldwell

The Evolution of Money

From Barter to Digital Currency

The Journey from Simplicity to Complexity

The history of money is as ancient as human civilization itself, beginning with the simple barter system, where goods were exchanged directly for other goods. This system, although effective in small, close-knit societies, quickly showed its limitations as communities expanded and trade became more complex. The need for a more efficient means of exchange led to the creation of money—a medium that could represent value and facilitate trade across different regions and cultures.

The Birth of Coinage

The first significant leap in the evolution of money was the introduction of coinage by the Lydians in the 7th century BCE. Made from electrum, a natural alloy of gold and silver, these coins were stamped with official marks to verify their weight and purity, setting a standard for value that transcended individual goods and services. This innovation revolutionized trade, enabling economic expansion and the development of more sophisticated financial systems.

Paper Money and the Concept of Trust

As economies grew, carrying large quantities of metal coins became impractical. The Chinese were among the first to adopt paper money during the Tang dynasty (618–907 AD), but it was during the Song dynasty (960–1279 AD) that this form of money became widespread. The transition from tangible coins to paper notes marked a pivotal shift towards a system based on trust—the trust that the paper represented a certain value and could be exchanged for goods or coins on demand.
The Digital Age and Electronic Money

The advent of the digital age brought about the next evolutionary step in the form of electronic money. Credit cards, wire transfers, and online banking transformed the way we access and spend our money, emphasizing convenience and speed. However, the reliance on banks and financial institutions as intermediaries has its drawbacks, including fees, privacy concerns, and the risk of censorship.

The Rise of Cryptocurrencies

The introduction of Bitcoin in 2009 by an individual or group using the pseudonym Satoshi Nakamoto marked the beginning of a new era in the evolution of money—cryptocurrencies. Cryptocurrencies are digital or virtual currencies that use cryptography for security and operate independently of a central bank. Bitcoin, and the many cryptocurrencies that followed, offer a decentralized alternative to traditional money, challenging the central authority of banks and governments.

Blockchain: The Technology Behind Cryptocurrencies

At the heart of Bitcoin and other cryptocurrencies lies blockchain technology—a decentralized ledger that records all transactions across a network of computers. Blockchain's transparency and security make it nearly impossible to alter historical data, addressing many of the trust issues inherent in traditional financial systems.

The Implications of Digital Currencies

The shift towards digital currencies is not just a technological change but a cultural and economic one. Cryptocurrencies offer the promise of a global financial system where anyone, regardless of their location or socio-economic status, can participate without the need for traditional banking infrastructure. This democratization of finance could lead to more equitable economic opportunities worldwide.

However, the rise of digital currencies also presents challenges, including regulatory concerns, market volatility, and the environmental impact of cryptocurrency mining. As we continue to navigate these issues, the evolution of money remains an ongoing journey—one that reflects our advancing technologies, changing economies, and the enduring quest for a more connected and efficient world.

Looking Ahead

As we stand on the brink of potential new advancements in money, such as Central Bank Digital Currencies (CBDCs) and further innovations in blockchain technology, it's clear that the evolution of money is far from over. The transition from barter to digital currency represents not just a change in the medium of exchange but a profound transformation in the way we conceive of and interact with value itself.

The Impact of Cryptocurrency on Global Finance

A New Era of Financial Independence

The advent of cryptocurrency has ushered in a revolutionary era in the global financial landscape, challenging traditional banking systems and redefining what we consider as money. With its roots deeply embedded in the desire for financial autonomy and privacy, cryptocurrency represents a pivotal shift towards a more decentralized and democratized financial system. This section explores the multifaceted impact of cryptocurrency on global finance, highlighting its potential to empower individuals, disrupt established financial institutions, and pave the way for innovative economic models.

Decentralization: Empowering the Unbanked

One of the most profound impacts of cryptocurrency is its ability to reach the unbanked and underbanked populations of the world. Traditional banking systems often exclude significant portions of the global population due to stringent requirements and geographical barriers. Cryptocurrencies, accessible to anyone with an internet connection, offer a lifeline, providing access to financial services without the need for a bank account. This inclusivity has the potential to empower millions, enabling them to participate in the global economy, invest, save, and secure their financial future.

Reducing Remittance Costs and Enhancing Efficiency

Cross-border remittances represent a crucial

financial lifeline for millions of families worldwide. However, the process is often slow and burdened with high fees. Cryptocurrencies have emerged as a game-changer in this domain, facilitating faster and more cost-effective international transfers. By leveraging blockchain technology, cryptocurrencies can significantly reduce transaction costs and processing times, making remittances more efficient and accessible to people worldwide.

Challenging Traditional Banking and Monetary Policy

Cryptocurrencies pose a direct challenge to the traditional banking system and the central authority of national monetary policies. By offering a decentralized alternative, they question the monopoly of central banks over money creation and control, potentially reducing the influence of government-imposed inflation or deflation. This shift introduces a new paradigm where monetary policy could become more democratic and less susceptible to manipulation or mismanagement by central authorities.

The Role of Privacy and Security

In an era where data breaches and financial surveillance are growing concerns, cryptocurrency offers an alternative that prioritizes user privacy and security. Transactions on the blockchain provide a level of anonymity and are secured by advanced cryptographic techniques, making them resistant to fraud and theft. This emphasis on privacy not only attracts individuals seeking to protect their financial transactions from prying eyes but also raises important questions about the balance between privacy and regulatory oversight.

Stimulating Financial Innovation and Competition

The rise of cryptocurrency has stimulated unprecedented levels of innovation in the financial sector. Fintech companies and startups are exploring new applications of blockchain technology, from creating more efficient payment systems to developing complex financial products that were previously unimaginable. This wave of innovation fosters competition, challenging traditional financial institutions to adapt and innovate or risk obsolescence.

Regulatory Challenges and the Path Forward

Despite its potential, the integration of cryptocurrency into the global financial system faces significant regulatory hurdles. Governments and financial regulators are grappling with how to classify, regulate, and tax cryptocurrency transactions while balancing the need for innovation with consumer protection and financial stability. The path forward requires a collaborative effort between the crypto community, regulators, and traditional financial institutions to establish a regulatory framework that supports innovation while safeguarding against risks.

Conclusion: A Transformative Force in Global Finance

Cryptocurrency stands at the forefront of a financial revolution, offering a vision of a more inclusive, efficient, and secure global financial system. Its impact extends beyond mere currency, challenging us to re-imagine the foundations of financial transactions and the role of trust in economic exchanges. As we continue to explore the possibilities and navigate the challenges, the ongoing evolution of cryptocurrency remains a testament to the human spirit's relentless pursuit of freedom, innovation, and financial empowerment.

Blockchain: The Backbone of Digital Finance

Understanding Blockchain Technology

The Foundation of a New Financial Era

At the heart of the digital finance revolution lies blockchain technology, a groundbreaking innovation that has emerged as the backbone of cryptocurrency and a myriad of other applications transforming the global financial landscape. This section delves into the fundamental concepts of blockchain, demystifying how it works and why it represents a pivotal shift in the way we perceive and manage financial transactions.

The Basics of Blockchain Technology

Blockchain is a distributed ledger technology (DLT) that records transactions across multiple computers in such a way that the registered transactions cannot be altered retroactively. This technology provides a secure and transparent way to conduct transactions without the need for a centralized authority, such as a bank or government. Each block in the blockchain contains a number of transactions; every time a new transaction occurs on the blockchain, a record of that transaction is added to every participant's ledger.

Decentralization: The Core Principle

The decentralized nature of blockchain is its defining characteristic. Unlike traditional financial systems, where a central entity controls the ledger, blockchain distributes the ledger across a network of computers (nodes). This decentralization ensures that no single entity has control over the entire network, making it more resistant to censorship, fraud, and failure.

Transparency and Security

Blockchain technology offers an unprecedented level of transparency and security. Transactions on the blockchain are visible to all participants and cannot be changed once they have been confirmed by the network. This transparency helps to build trust among users. Moreover, the use of cryptographic hashing and consensus algorithms ensures the integrity and security of transactions, making the blockchain remarkably resistant to hacking and tampering.

Smart Contracts: Automating Agreement

A significant innovation enabled by blockchain technology is the smart contract. Smart contracts are self-executing contracts with the terms of the agreement directly written into code. They automatically enforce and execute the terms of a contract when predetermined conditions are met, without the need for intermediaries. This automation has the potential to revolutionize various sectors by making transactions more efficient, transparent, and secure.

Blockchain Beyond Cryptocurrencies

While blockchain technology is most widely recognized for its role in powering cryptocurrencies, its potential applications extend far beyond. From supply chain management and healthcare to voting systems and identity verification, blockchain is paving the way for a host of decentralized applications (dApps) that promise to transform industries by enhancing transparency, security, and efficiency.

Challenges and Opportunities Ahead

Despite its numerous advantages, blockchain technology faces challenges, including scalability, energy consumption, and regulatory uncertainty. As the technology continues to evolve, solutions to these challenges are being developed, opening new opportunities for its application and adoption across various fields.

Conclusion: A Paradigm Shift in Finance and

Beyond

Understanding blockchain technology is essential to grasping the profound changes underway in the financial sector and beyond. As the backbone of digital finance, blockchain stands as a testament to the power of innovation to reshape the world, offering a glimpse into a future where transactions are more transparent, secure, and equitable. The journey of blockchain from a novel concept to a foundational technology underscores its potential to revolutionize not only finance but society as a whole, heralding a new era of decentralization and empowerment.

Blockchain Beyond Cryptocurrencies

Expanding Horizons: Blockchain's Versatile Applications

While blockchain technology is synonymous with cryptocurrencies, its potential extends far beyond the realms of digital finance. This versatile technology offers a foundation for trust and transparency, characteristics that are invaluable in various sectors. In this section, we explore the diverse applications of blockchain technology, demonstrating its impact on industries ranging from supply chain management to digital identity and beyond.

Supply Chain Management: Ensuring

Transparency and Trust

One of the most compelling uses of blockchain technology lies in supply chain management. By providing an immutable and transparent record of transactions, blockchain can track the movement of goods from origin to consumer, ensuring authenticity and reducing the likelihood of fraud. This capability is particularly beneficial in industries where provenance and transparency are critical, such as food safety, pharmaceuticals, and luxury goods. Through blockchain, stakeholders can verify the integrity of the supply chain, fostering trust among consumers and regulators alike.

Healthcare: Securing Patient Data and Enhancing Care

In the healthcare sector, blockchain offers solutions to some of the most pressing challenges, including data security, patient privacy, and interoperability of health records. By enabling secure, decentralized storage and sharing of medical records, blockchain technology can ensure patient data remains confidential while being accessible to authorized healthcare providers. This enhances the efficiency of diagnosis and treatment, reduces errors, and improves patient outcomes.

Digital Identity: A Gateway to Inclusion and Security

Digital identity is another area where blockchain technology can make a significant impact. With billions of people worldwide lacking official identification, blockchain can provide a secure and immutable digital identity, accessible via smartphones or computers. This innovation not only facilitates access to financial services, education, and healthcare but also enhances online security and privacy, reducing the risk of identity theft and fraud.

Real Estate and Land Registry: Simplifying Transactions and Ownership Verification

Blockchain technology is transforming the real estate sector by streamifying property transactions and land registry processes. By recording property ownership and transactions on a blockchain, all related information becomes easily verifiable and resistant to fraud. This can significantly reduce the time and cost associated with property transactions, making the market more accessible and transparent.

Voting Systems: Enhancing Integrity and Trust in Elections

Blockchain technology holds the promise of revolutionizing voting systems, making them more secure, transparent, and accessible. By recording votes on a blockchain, the technology can eliminate doubts about vote tampering and miscounts, ensuring the integrity of the electoral process. This application has the potential to increase voter turnout and trust in democratic processes, particularly in regions plagued by allegations of electoral fraud.

Intellectual Property and Content Management

For creators and artists, blockchain offers new ways to protect and monetize intellectual property.

By registering works on a blockchain, creators can ensure their ownership is securely and permanently recorded, facilitating copyright management and licensing. Furthermore, blockchain enables direct transactions between creators and consumers, potentially disrupting traditional media distribution models.

Challenges and the Path Forward

Despite its vast potential, the application of blockchain technology beyond cryptocurrencies faces challenges, including regulatory hurdles, technical limitations, and adoption barriers. Overcoming these challenges requires collaboration between technologists, industry stakeholders, and regulators to establish standards and frameworks that support innovation while ensuring security, privacy, and equity.

Conclusion: A World Transformed by Blockchain

Blockchain technology is set to redefine not only the financial sector but numerous industries worldwide. By offering unparalleled security, transparency, and efficiency, blockchain empowers individuals and organizations, paving the way for a more equitable and trustworthy digital future. As we explore and expand the applications of blockchain, we stand on the brink of a technological revolution that promises to transform society in profound and lasting ways.

The Surge of Decentralized Finance (DeFi)

Principles of DeFi

Redefining Finance: The Emergence of DeFi

Decentralized Finance, commonly known as DeFi, has emerged as a transformative force in the financial sector, challenging traditional banking and finance paradigms. Rooted in blockchain technology, DeFi extends the concept of decentralization to financial services, offering an open, accessible, and transparent alternative to conventional financial systems. This section delves into the core principles that underpin DeFi, elucidating how these principles catalyze innovation and empowerment in the financial domain.

Accessibility and Inclusivity

At the heart of DeFi lies the principle of accessibility. Unlike traditional finance, which often restricts access through regulatory and geographical barriers, DeFi platforms operate on a global scale, available to anyone with an internet connection. This inclusivity fosters financial empowerment by enabling individuals worldwide, including those in underserved or unbanked regions, to participate in financial markets and access services previously beyond their reach.

Transparency and Trust

DeFi stands on the pillars of transparency and trust, inherent to blockchain technology. All transactions within DeFi ecosystems are recorded on a public blockchain, allowing anyone to verify transactions and audit smart contracts. This level of transparency ensures that the operations of DeFi platforms are open and verifiable, building trust among users without the need for traditional trust intermediaries like banks.

Interoperability and Composability

Interoperability refers to the ability of different DeFi protocols and applications to work together seamlessly, while composability describes the capability to combine these elements to create new financial products or services. This "lego" nature of DeFi enables rapid innovation and customization, allowing developers and users to piece together different DeFi services and protocols to meet diverse financial needs.

Permissionless Innovation

DeFi is characterized by its permissionless nature, meaning that anyone can create, deploy, and use financial services on the blockchain. This open environment encourages innovation and competition, leading to the development of a wide array of financial instruments and services, from lending and borrowing platforms to synthetic assets and decentralized exchanges.

Self-Custody and Personal Responsibility

DeFi shifts the paradigm of custody in finance, empowering users to have direct control over their assets through the use of private keys and wallets. This self-custody model reduces the risk of centralized failures and fraud but also places greater responsibility on individuals to secure their assets and understand the risks involved in DeFi transactions.

Programmability and Automation

The programmability of DeFi, enabled by smart contracts, allows for the automation of financial transactions and agreements. This automation reduces the need for manual intervention, streamlining processes, and reducing costs. It also opens up possibilities for complex financial strategies that were either not possible or not economically viable in traditional finance.

Challenges and the Road Ahead

While DeFi's principles offer a vision of a more open, inclusive, and efficient financial system, challenges remain, including regulatory uncertainty, scalability issues, and the need for improved user interfaces. Overcoming these challenges requires ongoing innovation, community collaboration, and dialogue with regulators to ensure that DeFi can reach its full potential without compromising security or stability.

Conclusion: A Financial Revolution in the Making

The principles of DeFi represent a fundamental shift in the way we think about and interact with financial systems. By prioritizing accessibility, transparency, and innovation, DeFi has the potential to democratize finance, making it more equitable and efficient for all. As the DeFi ecosystem continues to evolve, it stands as a testament to the power of technology to transform not just finance, but society as a whole, paving the way for a future where financial services are by the people, for the people.

DeFi Platforms and Services

Navigating the DeFi Ecosystem

The decentralized finance (DeFi) ecosystem is vibrant and diverse, encompassing a wide range of platforms and services that redefine the landscape of financial services. From lending and borrowing markets to decentralized exchanges (DEXs) and yield farming opportunities, DeFi platforms leverage blockchain technology to offer financial instruments without the need for traditional intermediaries like banks. This section explores the variety of DeFi platforms and services, highlighting how they contribute to the financial empowerment of individuals globally.

Lending and Borrowing Platforms

One of the cornerstone services within the DeFi space is the provision of decentralized lending and borrowing. Platforms such as Compound and Aave allow users to lend their cryptocurrencies to earn interest or borrow against their digital assets as collateral. This peer-to-peer lending mechanism is facilitated by smart contracts, which automate the terms and ensure the security of transactions. These platforms have democratized access to lending and borrowing, providing users with flexible financial tools that were previously available only through traditional financial institutions.

Decentralized Exchanges (DEXs)

Decentralized exchanges represent another critical component of the DeFi ecosystem, offering a platform for the permissionless trading of cryptocurrencies without the need for a central authority. Unlike traditional exchanges, DEXs like Uniswap and SushiSwap facilitate direct trades between users' wallets through liquidity pools. This model not only enhances security and privacy by eliminating the need for users to deposit funds into a centralized exchange but also increases accessibility and market efficiency.

Yield Farming and Liquidity Mining

Yield farming, also known as liquidity mining, has emerged as a popular DeFi activity, where users lock up their assets in a DeFi protocol to earn rewards. The rewards, typically in the form of the protocol's native tokens, are incentives for providing liquidity to the platform's pools. This innovative mechanism has attracted significant capital into the DeFi space, driving the development of new financial products and strategies. Yield farming exemplifies the innovative and dynamic nature of DeFi, offering users the potential for high returns while contributing to the liquidity and stability of the DeFi market.

Stablecoins and Synthetic Assets

Stablecoins, such as DAI and USDC, play a pivotal role in the DeFi ecosystem by offering price stability amidst the volatility of the cryptocurrency market. These digital currencies are pegged to stable assets like the US dollar, providing a reliable medium of exchange for DeFi transactions. Beyond stablecoins, DeFi platforms also enable the creation of synthetic assets, which are blockchain-based representations of real-world assets, including stocks, commodities, or other cryptocurrencies. These instruments allow for greater market access and innovation within the DeFi space.

Insurance and Risk Management

As the DeFi ecosystem matures, platforms offering insurance and risk management solutions have become increasingly important. Protocols like Nexus Mutual provide coverage against smart contract failures, offering users a way to hedge against the inherent risks in the DeFi space. This development reflects the evolving nature of DeFi, as the community seeks to address the challenges and risks associated with decentralized financial services.

Challenges and the Path to Mainstream Adoption

While DeFi platforms and services offer a promising alternative to traditional finance, challenges such as scalability, user experience, and regulatory compliance must be addressed to facilitate broader adoption. Enhancing the scalability of blockchain networks, improving the intuitiveness of DeFi applications, and navigating the complex landscape of financial regulations are critical steps toward making DeFi accessible to a global audience.

Conclusion: A Diverse and Evolving Landscape

The DeFi ecosystem is rich and varied, offering a plethora of services that extend far beyond the capabilities of traditional financial systems. By leveraging blockchain technology and smart contracts, DeFi platforms provide a more accessible, transparent, and efficient financial landscape. As the DeFi space continues to evolve, it holds the promise of reshaping the global financial system, making it more inclusive and empowering for individuals worldwide.

Quantum Computing: Revolutionizing Finance

Basics of Quantum Computing in Finance

Introduction to Quantum Computing

Quantum computing represents a monumental leap forward in computational capabilities, harnessing the principles of quantum mechanics to process information in ways that traditional computers cannot. Unlike classical computing, which relies on bits (0s or 1s) to perform operations, quantum computing uses quantum bits, or qubits, which can exist in a state of 0, 1, or both simultaneously (superposition). This ability, along with quantum entanglement, allows quantum computers to perform complex calculations at unprecedented speeds.

Quantum Computing in Finance: A New Frontier

The financial sector, with its complex algorithms and vast datasets, stands to benefit significantly from quantum computing's advanced computational power. From optimizing portfolios and risk analysis to fraud detection and high-frequency trading, quantum computing promises to revolutionize various aspects of finance by offering solutions that are exponentially faster and more efficient than current methods.

Portfolio Optimization

Portfolio optimization is a fundamental challenge in finance, involving the selection of the best portfolio (asset distribution) out of a set of all possible portfolios, according to specific criteria. Quantum computing can enhance this process through its ability to quickly analyze and compute vast combinations of assets, considering various constraints and objectives. Quantum algorithms, such as the Quantum Approximate Optimization Algorithm (QAOA), could solve optimization problems more efficiently than classical algorithms, enabling investors to identify optimal asset allocations with unprecedented precision.

Risk Analysis and Management

Risk analysis and management are critical in finance, requiring the assessment of potential financial losses due to uncertainties in investment decisions. Quantum computing can significantly improve the accuracy and speed of risk calculations, such as Value at Risk (VaR) and Conditional Value at Risk (CVaR), by simulating numerous market scenarios and financial outcomes in parallel. This quantum-enhanced risk analysis could lead to more robust risk management strategies, helping financial institutions to better understand and mitigate potential losses.

Fraud Detection

Fraud detection involves identifying unauthorized financial activities, a task that requires the analysis of massive, complex datasets to spot irregularities and patterns indicative of fraud. Quantum computing's ability to process and analyze data at quantum speeds enables the detection of fraudulent activities more swiftly and accurately than traditional computing methods. Quantum algorithms could sift through transaction data in real-time, identifying anomalies that suggest fraudulent behavior, thus enhancing the security of financial systems.

High-frequency Trading (HFT)

High-frequency trading is a type of trading that uses powerful computer programs to transact a large number of orders in fractions of a second. Quantum computing could transform HFT by further reducing the time it takes to execute orders and analyze market data. The speed and efficiency of quantum algorithms would allow traders to exploit minute, fleeting arbitrage opportunities that are not accessible with classical computing techniques.

Challenges and Considerations

Despite its potential, the practical application of quantum computing in finance faces several challenges. Current quantum computers are in the early stages of development, with limitations in qubit stability (coherence time) and error rates that need to be overcome. Additionally, the development of quantum-resistant encryption methods is crucial to ensure that the increased computational power does not compromise the security of financial transactions and data.

The Road Ahead

As research and development in quantum computing continue to advance, its integration into the financial sector is expected to grow, offering transformative solutions to longstanding challenges. Financial institutions are already exploring quantum computing's potential, investing in research, and partnering with quantum technology companies to develop future applications. The journey towards fully realizing quantum computing's impact on finance is just beginning, promising a future where financial operations are more efficient, secure, and capable of handling the complexities of the global economy.

The Quantum Financial System (QFS)

A Glimpse into the Future of Finance

The concept of a Quantum Financial System (QFS) represents a futuristic vision for the financial industry, leveraging the unparalleled computational power of quantum computing to fundamentally transform how financial transactions and services are conducted, managed, and secured. While still theoretical, the QFS promises a financial infrastructure that is more secure, efficient, and transparent than ever before, potentially reshaping the global economy.

Understanding the Quantum Financial System

At its core, the Quantum Financial System is a proposed financial infrastructure that utilizes quantum computing technology to perform and secure financial transactions with unprecedented efficiency and security. The QFS is envisaged to harness the principles of quantum mechanics, particularly quantum entanglement and superposition, to facilitate instant, secure, and tamper-proof transactions across the globe.

Enhanced Security through Quantum Encryption

One of the most significant advantages of the QFS is its potential to revolutionize data security in financial transactions. Quantum encryption, or quantum key distribution (QKD), uses the principles of quantum mechanics to secure communication channels. Unlike traditional encryption methods that could potentially be broken by quantum computers, QKD is theoretically unbreakable, ensuring that financial transactions are immune to cyber threats and eavesdropping.

Instantaneous Global Transactions

The QFS could enable instantaneous financial transactions worldwide, regardless of the amount or the geographical location of the parties involved. This would be a monumental shift from the current financial system, where cross-border transactions can be slow and encumbered by various fees and regulatory requirements. The speed and efficiency of the QFS would support global trade and investment, fostering economic growth and development.

Decentralization and Reduced Intermediation

With the adoption of the QFS, the role of traditional financial intermediaries such as banks could be significantly diminished. Quantum computing technology could facilitate direct peer-to-peer transactions that are secure and instantaneous, reducing the need for intermediaries and potentially lowering transaction costs. This decentralization would not only democratize financial services but also increase their accessibility to underserved populations worldwide.

Challenges and Ethical Considerations
The transition to a Quantum Financial System poses significant technical, regulatory, and ethical challenges. The development of quantum-resistant cryptography is critical to protect against the potential misuse of quantum computing technology. Additionally, the implementation of the QFS would require global cooperation and consensus on standards, regulations, and protocols to ensure its secure and equitable use.

The potential impact of the QFS on employment within the financial sector, privacy concerns, and the digital divide between different regions and socioeconomic groups are also important ethical considerations that need to be addressed as part of its development and deployment.

The Path Forward

While the Quantum Financial System remains a concept rather than a current reality, its potential to revolutionize the financial industry is undeniable. As quantum computing technology continues to advance, the financial sector must prepare for the possibility of such transformative changes. This preparation involves investing in quantum research, developing new skills and competencies, and engaging in dialogue about the ethical and regulatory implications of quantum-powered finance.

Conclusion: Preparing for a Quantum-Powered Financial Future

The concept of the Quantum Financial System offers a tantalizing glimpse into the future of finance, where transactions are instantaneous, secure, and free from the limitations of today's financial infrastructure. While there are hurdles to overcome, the potential benefits of such a system—ranging from enhanced security to global financial inclusion—make it a compelling area for continued research and development. As the quantum era approaches, the financial industry must stay at the forefront of technological innovation, ensuring that it harnesses the power of quantum computing to create a more efficient, secure, and inclusive global economy.

Fintech Innovations: Bridging Technology and Finance

The Rise of Fintech

Revolutionizing the Financial Landscape

The financial industry has been undergoing a profound transformation, driven by the rapid advancement and integration of technology. This evolution has given rise to the fintech (financial technology) sector, a dynamic and innovative field that combines finance and technology to streamline, enhance, and democratize financial services. Fintech is not just about digitizing money; it's about creating new financial experiences, improving accessibility, and offering personalized services that were once the preserve of niche markets or large institutions.

Defining Fintech and Its Scope

Fintech encompasses a broad range of technologies, applications, and business models that impact the way financial operations are conducted and how financial services are delivered to consumers. It includes everything from mobile banking and peer-to-peer payment platforms to cryptocurrency, blockchain technology, and beyond. The goal is to make financial services more accessible, faster, and less expensive, catering to the digital-first preferences of modern consumers and businesses.

The Drivers Behind Fintech's Growth

Several factors have contributed to the meteoric rise of fintech, including:

- Technological Advancements: Innovations in AI, blockchain, and mobile technology have provided fintech companies with the tools to create groundbreaking services.
- Consumer Expectations: Today's consumers expect instant, on-demand access to financial services, driving demand for fintech solutions that offer convenience and user-friendly interfaces.
- Regulatory Changes: In many regions, regulatory frameworks have evolved to support fintech innovations, encouraging competition and fostering a more inclusive financial ecosystem.
- Global Connectivity: The internet and mobile technology have made it possible to deliver financial services across borders, opening up global markets to fintech innovations.

Impact on Traditional Banking and Finance

Fintech is reshaping the traditional banking and finance landscape, challenging incumbents to innovate and adapt. Banks and financial institutions are increasingly partnering with fintech companies or developing their own tech-driven solutions to meet changing consumer demands. This collaboration between traditional finance and fintech is creating a hybrid model where technology enhances the efficiency and reach of financial services.

Fintech's Role in Financial Inclusion

One of the most significant impacts of fintech is its potential to increase financial inclusion. By leveraging technology, fintech companies can provide financial services to underserved and unbanked populations around the world. Mobile banking, microfinance, and digital payment platforms offer a lifeline to those without access to traditional banking, contributing to economic empowerment and poverty reduction.

The Future of Fintech

As fintech continues to evolve, it is set to further disrupt the financial sector with emerging technologies like AI-driven financial advisory, decentralized finance (DeFi), and programmable money. The future of fintech lies in its ability to blend technology seamlessly with finance, creating a more inclusive, efficient, and secure global financial system.

Challenges and Opportunities Ahead

Despite its promising growth, the fintech sector faces challenges, including regulatory hurdles, cybersecurity threats, and the need for continuous innovation to stay ahead in a competitive market. However, these challenges also present opportunities for growth and development, pushing the fintech sector to innovate and improve continually.

Conclusion: A New Era of Financial Services

The rise of fintech marks the beginning of a new era in financial services, characterized by innovation, inclusivity, and efficiency. As technology continues to advance, the boundaries of what is possible in finance expand, promising a future where financial services are accessible to all, tailored to individual needs, and seamlessly integrated into our digital lives. Fintech not only represents the future of finance but also reflects a broader shift towards a more equitable and technology-driven world.

Fintech Solutions for a Better World

Empowering Societies Through Financial Technology

Fintech, or financial technology, has rapidly

evolved from a disruptive force to a foundational element in the modern financial landscape, offering solutions that extend far beyond mere convenience. This sector's innovative approaches are now addressing some of the most pressing global challenges, including financial inclusion, economic empowerment, and sustainable development. In this section, we delve into how fintech is being leveraged to create a better world, highlighting its role in promoting inclusivity, efficiency, and resilience in financial systems worldwide.

Financial Inclusion: Breaking Down Barriers

One of Fintech's most profound impacts has been its ability to enhance financial inclusion, providing access to financial services for populations traditionally excluded from the formal banking system. Through mobile banking apps, digital wallets, and micro-lending platforms, fintech has opened the doors to banking, saving, and borrowing for millions of unbanked and underbanked individuals around the globe. These technologies empower people in remote or impoverished regions, offering them tools for economic participation and growth.

Digital Banking Services: A Gateway to Economic Participation

Fintech has also revolutionized the concept of banking itself, with digital banking services offering user-friendly, accessible financial management tools. From setting up an account with just a few clicks to managing finances through intuitive apps, digital banking has made financial management more accessible and understandable for the general public. This democratization of financial services encourages a more financially literate society, equipped to make informed decisions about their economic well-being.

Peer-to-Peer Lending: Democratizing Access to Capital

Peer-to-peer (P2P) lending platforms exemplify Fintech's role in democratizing access to capital. By connecting borrowers directly with lenders, these platforms bypass traditional financial intermediaries, often resulting in lower interest rates for borrowers and higher returns for investors. This model has proven particularly beneficial for small and medium-sized enterprises (SMEs) and entrepreneurs, who may struggle to secure funding from conventional sources, thereby fostering innovation, job creation, and economic diversity.

Sustainable Finance: Aligning Investments with Global Goals

Fintech is at the forefront of the sustainable finance movement, harnessing technology to align investments with environmental, social, and governance (ESG) criteria. Through platforms that offer green bonds, ESG investing, and impact investing opportunities, fintech enables individuals and institutions to invest in projects that contribute to a sustainable future. This not only provides financial returns but also supports the global transition towards sustainability and responsible business practices.

Blockchain for Transparency and Accountability

Blockchain technology, a cornerstone of fintech, has emerged as a powerful tool for enhancing transparency and accountability in financial transactions and beyond. By providing an immutable, decentralized ledger for recording transactions, blockchain can help combat fraud, corruption, and misuse of funds in both the public and private sectors. Its applications range from tracking the provenance of goods in supply chains to ensuring the integrity of charitable donations and public funds.

Challenges to Overcome

While fintech offers promising solutions for a better world, it also faces challenges that must be addressed to realize its full potential. Regulatory hurdles, digital divide issues, and concerns about data privacy and security are among the key obstacles. Fostering collaboration between fintech firms, regulators, and traditional financial institutions, along with investing in digital literacy and infrastructure, will be crucial in overcoming these challenges.

Conclusion: A Catalyst for Positive Change

Fintech solutions have the potential to reshape the world's financial landscape, making it more inclusive, efficient, and sustainable. By leveraging technology to address critical global challenges, fintech stands as a catalyst for positive change, driving social and economic progress. As the sector continues to evolve, its role in building a better world for future generations will undoubtedly expand, highlighting the importance of innovation, collaboration, and regulation in harnessing the full power of financial technology.

Rethinking Investment in the 21st Century

Modern Investment Strategies

Adapting to a Rapidly Changing World

The landscape of investment has undergone significant transformations in the 21st century, driven by globalization, technological advancements, and shifts in economic power. These changes have not only influenced the types of investment vehicles available but have also led to the development of modern investment strategies that are adaptive, diversified, and technologically savvy. This section explores how investors are navigating this new terrain, leveraging innovative approaches to maximize returns while managing risk in a volatile global market.

The Shift Towards Diversification

One of the fundamental tenets of modern investment strategies is diversification. The adage "don't put all your eggs in one basket" has never been more relevant, as investors seek to spread their capital across various asset classes, industries, and geographies to mitigate risk. Diversification can protect investors from market volatility and unforeseen economic downturns, ensuring more stable returns over the long term.

Leveraging Technology for Investment Analysis

Technological advancements have profoundly impacted modern investment strategies. Big data analytics, artificial intelligence (AI), and machine learning are now integral tools for analyzing market trends, assessing risks, and identifying investment opportunities. These technologies enable investors to process vast amounts of information rapidly, providing insights that were previously inaccessible and allowing for more informed decision-making.

Sustainable and Responsible Investing (SRI)

Sustainable and Responsible Investing has gained traction among modern investors who seek not only financial returns but also positive societal impact. SRI involves investing in companies that adhere to environmental, social, and governance (ESG) criteria, reflecting a broader trend towards ethical investing. Investors are increasingly recognizing that companies committed to sustainability and ethical practices often exhibit stronger financial performance and resilience, making SRI a strategic investment approach for the 21st century.

The Emergence of Alternative Investments

The search for higher returns and lower correlations with traditional markets has led investors towards alternative investments, including private equity, hedge funds, real estate, commodities, and cryptocurrencies. These alternatives can offer unique benefits, such as inflation protection and diversification, but they also come with higher risks and liquidity concerns. Understanding these complexities is crucial for modern investors aiming to incorporate alternative assets into their portfolios effectively.

The Role of Robo-Advisors in Personal Investment

Robo-advisors, automated digital platforms that provide tailored investment advice based on algorithms, have democratized access to investment management. By offering low-cost, personalized portfolio management services, robo-advisors appeal to a wide range of investors, from novices seeking to enter the market to seasoned investors looking to optimize their portfolios. This shift towards digital advisory services represents a significant evolution in personal investment strategies.

Navigating Market Volatility with Tactical Asset Allocation

Modern investment strategies often involve tactical asset allocation, a dynamic approach that adjusts the mix of assets in a portfolio in response to short-term market conditions and opportunities. Unlike a strictly passive strategy, tactical asset allocation allows investors to capitalize on market trends and economic indicators, potentially enhancing returns while managing risk.

Conclusion: A New Paradigm for Investors

The 21st century has introduced a new paradigm for investors, characterized by rapid technological change, evolving market dynamics, and a growing emphasis on sustainability and ethics. Modern investment strategies reflect these shifts, prioritizing diversification, technological integration, and a more nuanced approach to risk management. As investors continue to navigate this complex landscape, adaptability, informed decision-making, and a commitment to learning will be key to achieving long-term financial success.

Cryptocurrencies and Blockchain in Investment

A Digital Revolution in Asset Management

The advent of cryptocurrencies and blockchain

technology has ignited a digital revolution in the world of investment, introducing assets that are fundamentally different from traditional stocks, bonds, and commodities. This section delves into the burgeoning role of cryptocurrencies and blockchain in modern investment strategies, exploring how these digital assets are reshaping investor portfolios and offering new opportunities and challenges in asset management.

Cryptocurrencies: The New Frontier in Investing

Cryptocurrencies, led by Bitcoin, have emerged as a new asset class that offers a combination of currency and investment attributes. Unlike fiat currencies, cryptocurrencies operate on decentralized blockchain networks, offering a level of transparency, security, and resistance to censorship unmatched by traditional financial systems. The volatile nature of cryptocurrencies can lead to significant returns, but it also involves substantial risk, making them a contentious yet intriguing option for investors seeking to diversify their portfolios.

Blockchain: More Than Just Cryptocurrency

While blockchain technology is the foundation of cryptocurrencies, its potential applications in investment extend far beyond digital currencies. Blockchain can streamline and secure the process of buying, selling, and trading assets through smart contracts and decentralized finance (DeFi) platforms. These technologies can reduce transaction costs, improve efficiency, and enhance transparency in investment operations, from real estate transactions to equity trading.

Integrating Cryptocurrencies into Diversified Portfolios

As institutional and retail interest in cryptocurrencies grows, investors are increasingly considering how to integrate these digital assets into their diversified portfolios. Strategies vary from allocating a small percentage of the portfolio to cryptocurrencies as a hedge against inflation and currency devaluation to actively trading cryptocurrencies to capitalize on their volatility. The key to integrating cryptocurrencies effectively lies in understanding their market dynamics, regulatory environment, and potential impact on portfolio risk and return.

The Rise of Tokenization and Digital Assets

Blockchain technology has facilitated the tokenization of traditional assets, such as real estate, art, and commodities, creating digital tokens that represent ownership or a share in the underlying asset. This process democratizes access to investments that were previously illiquid or inaccessible to average investors, allowing for fractional ownership, increased liquidity, and a broader distribution of investment opportunities.

DeFi: An Ecosystem of Financial Innovation
The decentralized finance (DeFi) ecosystem, built on blockchain technology, has introduced a range of innovative financial services that challenge traditional investment and banking paradigms. From yield farming and liquidity mining to decentralized lending and borrowing platforms, DeFi offers investors novel ways to generate returns on their digital asset holdings. However, the nascent nature of DeFi, along with its regulatory uncertainty and operational risks, requires careful navigation.

Challenges and Considerations

Investing in cryptocurrencies and blockchain technology presents a unique set of challenges, including regulatory uncertainty, market volatility, and security risks associated with hacking and fraud. Investors must conduct thorough due diligence, stay informed about technological and regulatory developments, and consider the implications of digital assets on their investment strategy and risk tolerance.

Conclusion: Embracing the Digital Investment Era

The integration of cryptocurrencies and

blockchain into investment strategies marks a significant shift towards a more digital, decentralized, and dynamic financial landscape. While the risks associated with these digital assets are non-negligible, their potential to offer diversification, innovation, and enhanced returns makes them an increasingly important component of 21st-century investment portfolios. As the technology matures and regulatory frameworks evolve, cryptocurrencies and blockchain could become integral to the future of investment.

The Future of Transactions: Beyond Cash

Towards a Cashless Society

The Evolution of Money in the Digital Age

As the world progresses into the digital age, the concept of a cashless society, where physical money is replaced by digital transactions, is becoming increasingly plausible. This transition towards digital payments is driven by a combination of technological advancements, changing consumer preferences, and the push from governments and financial institutions for more efficient, secure, and inclusive financial systems. In this section, we explore the drivers behind the move towards a cashless society and the implications for individuals, businesses, and economies worldwide.

Technological Innovations Fueling the Cashless Movement

The foundation of the cashless society is the array of technological innovations that have made digital transactions convenient, secure, and fast. Mobile payments, online banking, digital wallets, and contactless cards are at the forefront of this transformation, offering users a level of convenience that cash cannot match. The proliferation of smartphones has further accelerated this trend, enabling instant payments and financial services accessible from anywhere at any time.

The Benefits of Going Cashless

A cashless society promises numerous benefits, including enhanced transaction efficiency, reduced risk of theft and fraud, and lower transaction costs for businesses. Digital transactions can be tracked and recorded, simplifying budgeting and financial management for consumers and improving transparency and accountability in financial systems. Moreover, digital payments play a crucial role in financial inclusion, offering access to financial services for populations previously underserved by traditional banking systems.

Global Trends Towards Cashless Transactions

Various countries around the world are at different stages of transitioning to cashless economies, with nations like Sweden, South Korea, and China leading the way. These countries have seen a significant decline in cash usage as digital payment methods become ubiquitous in retail, transportation, and even person-to-person transactions. Government initiatives, such as India's demonetization effort and the promotion of digital payments, highlight the push towards reducing reliance on cash.

Challenges and Concerns

Despite the advantages, the move towards a cashless society raises several challenges and concerns. Privacy and security issues emerge as financial transactions become entirely digital, increasing the potential for cyberattacks and data breaches. There is also the risk of excluding those without access to digital technology or banking services, such as the elderly or people in rural areas, potentially widening the digital divide.

Additionally, the reliance on technology and the internet for financial transactions introduces vulnerabilities, including system failures and power outages, that could disrupt economic activities.

Navigating the Transition

The transition to a cashless society requires careful navigation to balance the benefits of digital payments with the need to address privacy, security, and inclusivity concerns. Policymakers, financial institutions, and technology providers must collaborate to create regulatory frameworks, invest in secure and resilient infrastructure, and ensure that digital financial services are accessible and inclusive. Education and digital literacy programs are essential to prepare all segments of society for a future where cash is no longer king.

Conclusion: Embracing a Digital Financial Future

The journey towards a cashless society is well underway, propelled by technological advancements and changing consumer behaviors. While this transition offers the promise of a more efficient, secure, and inclusive financial system, it also necessitates a comprehensive approach to address the associated challenges. By fostering innovation, ensuring robust security measures, and promoting inclusivity, the vision of a cashless society can be realized, marking a significant milestone in the evolution of money and transactions in the digital age.

Security and Privacy in Digital Transactions

Safeguarding the Digital Economy

The shift towards a cashless society brings with it the paramount importance of security and privacy in digital transactions. As financial interactions become increasingly digital, the potential for cyber threats, data breaches, and privacy violations escalates, raising concerns among consumers, businesses, and regulators alike. This section delves into the challenges of ensuring security and privacy in a digital financial ecosystem and explores the measures and technologies being developed to protect users in the evolving landscape of digital transactions.

The Landscape of Digital Security Threats

The digital finance ecosystem is continuously under threat from cybercriminals exploiting vulnerabilities for financial gain. Phishing attacks, identity theft, and unauthorized access to financial accounts are just a few examples of the risks associated with digital transactions. The sophistication of these threats requires equally advanced security solutions to protect sensitive financial data and maintain consumer trust in digital financial services.

Enhancing Security Measures

To combat the evolving threats, a multi-layered approach to security is essential. Encryption technologies, such as SSL (Secure Socket Layer) and TLS (Transport Layer Security), play a critical role in securing data transmission over the internet. Two-factor authentication (2FA) and biometric verification, including fingerprint and facial recognition, add additional layers of security, verifying the identity of users and mitigating the risk of unauthorized access.

Blockchain: A Paradigm Shift in Transaction Security

Blockchain technology is emerging as a transformative solution for enhancing security in digital transactions. By providing a decentralized and tamper-proof ledger for recording transactions, blockchain technology can prevent fraud and ensure the integrity of financial data. The use of smart contracts—self-executing contracts with the terms directly written into code—further automates and secures financial agreements, reducing the potential for disputes and malfeasance.

Privacy Concerns in a Digital World

While security focuses on protecting data from unauthorized access, privacy ensures that individuals' financial information is used and shared ethically and in accordance with their preferences. The challenge of maintaining privacy in digital transactions lies in balancing the need for security and regulatory compliance with individuals' rights to data protection. Technologies such as privacy-enhancing cryptography and secure multi-party computation are being explored to enable the processing of transactions without exposing sensitive data.

Regulatory Frameworks and Consumer Protection

Governments and regulatory bodies worldwide are responding to the security and privacy challenges of digital transactions by implementing stringent data protection laws and financial regulations. The General Data Protection Regulation (GDPR) in the European Union and the Payment Card Industry Data Security Standard (PCI DSS) globally are examples of regulatory efforts to protect consumers in the digital age. These regulations mandate strict security measures and grant individuals greater control over their personal data, setting the standard for privacy and security in digital finance.

The Future of Digital Transaction Security

As the financial ecosystem continues to evolve, the development of advanced security technologies and privacy-preserving mechanisms will be crucial in safeguarding the future of transactions. Innovations in artificial intelligence, machine learning, and quantum cryptography hold the promise of enhancing the detection and prevention of security threats, ensuring the resilience of digital financial services. Moreover, fostering a culture of security and privacy awareness among consumers and businesses is essential for building a secure and trustworthy digital economy.

Conclusion: Navigating the Digital Frontier

The transition to a cashless society underscores the critical importance of security and privacy in digital transactions. By adopting advanced security measures, exploring innovative technologies, and adhering to robust regulatory standards, the financial industry can protect consumers and businesses from cyber threats and privacy violations. As we navigate the digital frontier, the collective efforts of technology providers, financial institutions, regulators, and users will determine the success of our journey towards a secure and privacy-respecting digital financial ecosystem.

The Role of American Patriotism in Finance

Patriotism and Economic Policies

A Fusion of National Identity and Economic Strategy

The intertwining of American patriotism and economic policy is a profound testament to the nation's enduring spirit and its pursuit of prosperity and security. This relationship is rooted in the belief that economic strength is a cornerstone of national sovereignty and global leadership. By examining the impact of patriotism on economic policies, we can understand how the United States leverages its economic might to uphold its values and interests on the global stage.

Historical Perspectives on Economic Patriotism

The concept of economic patriotism in the United States has historical roots dating back to the founding fathers, who emphasized the importance of financial independence and self-sufficiency for the nascent nation. From Alexander Hamilton's advocacy for a strong central bank and manufacturing base to the protectionist policies of the early 20th century, American economic policies have often been guided by the principle of bolstering national interests and security.

Modern Manifestations of Economic Patriotism

In contemporary times, economic patriotism manifests through policies designed to protect and promote American industries, labor, and technological advancements. This includes tariffs on imported goods, subsidies for domestic industries, and stringent regulations on foreign investments in critical sectors. Such measures are often justified as necessary to protect national security, maintain economic sovereignty, and preserve American jobs and manufacturing capabilities.

The Role of Economic Sanctions and Trade Agreements

Economic patriotism also extends to the use of economic sanctions and trade agreements as tools of foreign policy. By imposing sanctions on countries that threaten its interests or violate international norms, the United States leverages its economic power to achieve diplomatic objectives without resorting to military action. Similarly, trade agreements are negotiated to ensure that they reflect American values and interests, promoting fair trade practices and opening markets for American goods and services.

Innovation and Technological Superiority as Patriotic Endeavors

The pursuit of technological superiority is another aspect of economic patriotism, with the government investing heavily in research and development in areas such as defense, space exploration, and information technology. These investments are seen as vital to maintaining America's competitive edge and leadership in the global economy. The narrative of innovation is often framed as a patriotic endeavor, with American ingenuity and entrepreneurship celebrated as key contributors to national strength and prosperity.

Balancing Economic Patriotism and Global Interdependence

While economic patriotism emphasizes national interests, it must also contend with the realities of global interdependence. The challenge lies in crafting policies that protect American economic interests without alienating allies or disrupting international trade and cooperation. This balancing act is crucial in an era where economic challenges are increasingly global in nature, requiring coordinated responses across borders.

Conclusion: Patriotism as a Guiding Principle in Economic Policy

Economic patriotism in the United States is a reflection of a broader commitment to safeguarding the nation's prosperity, security, and values through strategic economic policies. By aligning economic initiatives with patriotic principles, the United States seeks to navigate the complexities of the global economy while reinforcing its position as a world leader. As the global economic landscape continues to evolve, the role of patriotism in shaping economic policy remains a dynamic and influential force in American governance and society.

National Pride and Financial Innovation

Cultivating Innovation within the Fabric of American Identity

The fusion of national pride and financial innovation in the United States underscores a unique aspect of American patriotism — its deep-seated belief in the power of innovation to drive progress, prosperity, and global leadership. This chapter delves into how American patriotism has not only fostered a conducive environment for financial innovation but also how such advancements have, in turn, become a source of national pride and a tool for strengthening the country's economic sovereignty.

The American Dream: A Catalyst for Financial Innovation

At the heart of American patriotism lies the American Dream, the ideal that every individual has the opportunity for prosperity and success through hard work and innovation. This ethos has been a driving force behind the country's vibrant culture of entrepreneurship and innovation, particularly in the financial sector. Innovations ranging from the creation of the modern credit system to the development of complex financial instruments and technology-driven platforms reflect the American spirit of ingenuity and the pursuit of progress.

Silicon Valley and the Tech-Driven Financial Sector

Silicon Valley, a symbol of American innovation and technological prowess, has played a pivotal role in reshaping the financial landscape through the emergence of fintech (financial technology) companies. These entities have revolutionized how financial services are delivered, making them more accessible, efficient, and secure. The success of fintech startups has not only contributed to the U.S. economy but has also become a source of national pride, showcasing America's ability to lead in the creation of cutting-edge technologies.

Government Support for Financial Innovation

The United States government has historically recognized the importance of innovation in maintaining economic competitiveness and national security. Through various initiatives and policies, such as research and development tax credits, grants, and regulatory sandboxes, the government has provided a supportive ecosystem for financial innovation. This backing underscores the patriotic view that fostering innovation is integral to the country's continued prosperity and leadership on the global stage.

The Global Influence of American Financial Innovations

American financial innovations have had a profound impact on the global financial system, from the widespread adoption of the dollar as the world's primary reserve currency to the influence of Wall Street as a global financial center. The export of financial products, services, and regulatory frameworks developed in the United States has further cemented its status as a leader in financial innovation, contributing to the country's soft power and international influence.

Challenges and Ethical Considerations

While the pursuit of financial innovation is a

source of national pride, it also presents challenges and ethical considerations, such as the need to balance innovation with consumer protection and financial stability. The rapid pace of technological change and the complexity of new financial products can pose risks to both individuals and the broader financial system. Addressing these challenges requires a commitment to responsible innovation and the development of robust regulatory frameworks.

Conclusion: Financial Innovation as a Pillar of American Patriotism

National pride and financial innovation are deeply intertwined in the American consciousness, reflecting a collective belief in the power of ingenuity to foster economic growth and enhance the country's standing in the world. As the United States continues to navigate the complexities of the global economy, the spirit of innovation, supported by a patriotic commitment to progress and prosperity, will remain a defining feature of its financial sector and a key driver of its economic policy.

Economic Freedom and Liberty

The Philosophy of Economic Freedom

Understanding Economic Freedom

Economic freedom stands as a fundamental principle that underpins the prosperity, innovation, and democratic values of societies. It embodies the right of individuals to choose how to produce, consume, and exchange goods and services in a free market, with minimal government intervention. This chapter explores the philosophy of economic freedom, its significance in fostering liberty and prosperity, and the role it plays in shaping the economic policies and practices of nations.

Historical Foundations and Theoretical Perspectives

The philosophy of economic freedom is deeply rooted in classical liberal thought, dating back to thinkers like Adam Smith, John Locke, and Friedrich Hayek. These philosophers argued that economic freedom is intrinsically linked to individual liberty, positing that a free market economy is the most efficient and just way to allocate resources. According to this view, when individuals are free to pursue their economic interests, it leads to innovation, economic growth, and an overall increase in societal well-being.

Economic Freedom and Its Dimensions

Economic freedom encompasses several key dimensions, including personal choice, voluntary exchange, freedom to enter and compete in markets, and security of privately owned property. Each of these dimensions contributes to the overall economic freedom of a country and its citizens, facilitating a dynamic and resilient economy. Countries that score high on indices of economic freedom typically exhibit strong economic growth, higher standards of living, and greater political and civil liberties.

The Impact of Economic Freedom on Prosperity

Empirical evidence consistently demonstrates a positive correlation between economic freedom and various indicators of economic prosperity. Nations with higher degrees of economic freedom enjoy higher GDP per capita, better health outcomes, higher levels of education, and lower incidences of poverty. The freedom to innovate, start businesses, and trade openly with others fosters an environment where creativity and efficiency flourish, driving economic development and improving quality of life.

Challenges to Economic Freedom

Despite its benefits, economic freedom faces challenges from various quarters, including government regulations, corruption, and protectionist policies. Excessive government intervention in the economy can stifle innovation, lead to inefficiencies, and curtail individual liberties. Likewise, corruption undermines economic freedom by distorting market mechanisms and diverting resources away from productive uses. Advocates of economic freedom argue for the importance of rule of law, transparent governance, and open markets as foundational to preserving and enhancing economic liberty.

Balancing Economic Freedom with Social Responsibilities

The pursuit of economic freedom must be balanced with considerations of equity and social justice. Critics of unfettered markets highlight the risks of inequality and exploitation in the absence of regulatory safeguards. A balanced approach advocates for a regulatory framework that protects individual rights and property while ensuring that the benefits of economic freedom are widely shared across society. This includes policies that promote access to education, healthcare, and opportunities for economic participation.

Conclusion: The Path Forward for Economic
Freedom

The philosophy of economic freedom serves as a
guiding principle for nations striving to achieve
prosperity and liberty. As societies navigate the
complexities of the global economy, the challenge
lies in fostering an environment that maximizes
economic freedom while ensuring fairness and
security for all citizens. By embracing the
principles of economic freedom, societies can
unleash the potential of individuals and
businesses, driving innovation and progress in the
pursuit of a more prosperous and free world.

Challenges to Economic Freedom

Navigating the Complex Terrain of Modern
Economies

While economic freedom is heralded for its ability
to drive prosperity and innovation, it faces a
myriad of challenges in the contemporary world.
These obstacles not only threaten the principles of
liberty and free market dynamics but also pose
significant questions about the sustainability and
fairness of economic systems. This section delves
into the primary challenges to economic freedom
today, examining their implications and the
strategies needed to address them.

Regulatory Constraints and Government Intervention

One of the most significant challenges to economic freedom is the tendency towards increased government intervention and regulatory constraints. While regulations are necessary for protecting consumers, ensuring fair competition, and safeguarding the environment, excessive or poorly designed regulations can stifle entrepreneurship, reduce efficiency, and limit individual economic choice. Finding the right balance between regulation and freedom is a continuous challenge for policymakers.

Globalization and Sovereignty

Globalization has brought about unprecedented economic integration, offering numerous benefits, including access to broader markets, diversification of resources, and acceleration of innovation. However, it also raises concerns about economic sovereignty and the ability of nations to control their economic policies. The tension between benefiting from global markets and maintaining economic independence is a delicate balancing act for countries striving to preserve their economic freedom.

Income Inequality and Social Equity

Another challenge facing economic freedom is the issue of income inequality and its impact on social equity. Critics argue that unchecked free markets can lead to significant disparities in wealth and access to opportunities, undermining social cohesion and stability. Addressing these concerns without impeding economic freedom requires thoughtful policies that promote equality of opportunity, such as investments in education, healthcare, and infrastructure, while encouraging economic participation and innovation.

Technological Advancements and Labor Markets

The rapid pace of technological change, while a driver of economic growth, presents challenges to economic freedom, particularly in labor markets. Automation and digitization can displace workers and exacerbate job insecurity, posing questions about the future of work and the role of government in supporting affected individuals. Adapting to these changes necessitates policies that foster skills development, lifelong learning, and mobility in the workforce.

Financial Markets and Stability

Financial markets are integral to a free economy, facilitating investment, consumption, and risk management. However, financial crises have highlighted the vulnerabilities within these markets and the catastrophic impact they can have on economies. Ensuring financial market stability while maintaining economic freedom requires robust regulatory frameworks that prevent excessive risk-taking and ensure transparency and accountability.

Environmental Sustainability

The challenge of environmental sustainability intersects with economic freedom, as unrestricted economic activities can lead to environmental degradation. Balancing economic growth with environmental stewardship necessitates innovative approaches that leverage market mechanisms to promote sustainable practices, such as carbon pricing and green technologies, without overly restrictive regulations that could hamper economic dynamism.

Conclusion: Fortifying Economic Freedom Amid Challenges

The path to sustaining economic freedom amid these challenges is complex but not insurmountable. It requires a nuanced approach that values the principles of freedom while recognizing the need for responsible governance, social equity, and environmental stewardship. By fostering open dialogue, encouraging innovation, and pursuing policies that balance individual liberty with the common good, societies can navigate these challenges and ensure that economic freedom remains a cornerstone of prosperity and progress.

NESARA/GESARA: Myths and Realities

The Origins and Objectives of NESARA/GESARA

Unveiling the Mythical Layers

The concepts of the National Economic Security and Reformation Act (NESARA) and the Global Economic Security and Reformation Act (GESARA) have circulated within certain fringe and conspiracy theory groups for years. Ostensibly aimed at transforming economic and social systems through a series of sweeping reforms, these proposals have been the subject of much speculation, misinformation, and hope among their proponents. This section aims to dissect the origins, alleged objectives, and the blend of fact and fiction surrounding NESARA and GESARA, providing a clear perspective on these controversial and widely misunderstood concepts. Historical Origins of NESARA

The origins of NESARA can be traced back to the late 1990s, with a proposal put forward by Harvey Francis Barnard, an engineer and educator from Louisiana. Barnard's NESARA was initially a set of economic reforms focused on eliminating debt, reorganizing tax structures, and increasing transparency in financial and governmental institutions. Barnard's proposal sought to address systemic inequalities and inefficiencies within the U.S. economy, proposing radical solutions such as the abolition of the Federal Reserve System, the introduction of a flat tax system, and the return to a bimetallic currency standard.

The Evolution into a Conspiracy Theory

Over time, NESARA evolved from a proposal for economic reform into a full-fledged conspiracy theory, with claims that the act had been secretly passed by the U.S. Congress and was being suppressed by global elites. According to these conspiracy narratives, NESARA's implementation would usher in an era of peace, prosperity, and global financial reset, abolishing personal debts and redistributing wealth. The theory also intertwines with other conspiracies, including those related to extraterrestrial involvement in government affairs and the existence of a deep state.

The Concept of GESARA

Expanding on the foundations of NESARA, the concept of GESARA extends the idea to a global scale, proposing a worldwide economic reset that would eliminate poverty, ensure environmental sustainability, and foster global peace. According to proponents, GESARA would lead to significant changes in governance and financial systems across the world, including the dissolution of institutions like the United Nations and the International Monetary Fund, the establishment of universal basic income, and the adoption of a global currency.

Analyzing the Objectives

The purported objectives of NESARA and GESARA touch on genuine concerns about economic inequality, environmental degradation, and the concentration of power in the hands of a few. However, the solutions proposed by these concepts are often unrealistic and not grounded in practical economic or political theory. The sweeping reforms suggested lack a clear implementation strategy and fail to address the complexities of global finance and governance.

The Impact of the Myth

Despite the lack of evidence supporting the existence or feasibility of NESARA and GESARA, the myths surrounding them have garnered a significant following. They reflect a deep-seated desire for systemic change and a more equitable society. However, the dissemination of these myths can also divert attention from viable policy discussions and reforms, leading individuals to place their hopes in unattainable solutions.

Conclusion: Separating Fact from Fiction

Understanding NESARA and GESARA requires a discerning look at their origins, objectives, and the context in which they have evolved. While the allure of simple solutions to complex problems is understandable, it is essential to ground discussions of economic and social reform in reality, focusing on actionable and sustainable approaches. By separating fact from fiction, we can engage in meaningful debates on how to address the pressing challenges facing our economies and societies.

Economic Reforms for Global Prosperity

Envisioning a Framework for Sustainable Change

While the specific proposals of NESARA and GESARA as they are popularly understood may not be grounded in reality, the underlying desire for comprehensive economic reform and global prosperity that these concepts symbolize is both real and widespread. This section explores the idea of implementing viable economic reforms aimed at achieving global prosperity, drawing on some of the themes associated with NESARA/GESARA but focusing on actionable and realistic strategies.

Addressing Economic Inequality

One of the core objectives often associated with
NESARA/GESARA is the reduction of economic
inequality. Real-world strategies to address this
issue include progressive taxation, enhanced social
safety nets, and increased access to education and
healthcare. These measures can help ensure that
economic growth benefits a broader segment of
the population, reducing poverty and improving
overall societal well-being.

Debt Relief and Financial Stability

The idea of debt relief, another theme common to
NESARA/GESARA narratives, can be applied
pragmatically through policies that restructure or
forgive unsustainable debt for individuals and
nations alike. For countries, particularly those in
the developing world, debt relief initiatives can
free up resources for investment in critical
infrastructure, education, and healthcare, fostering
economic stability and growth.

Sustainable Development and Environmental
Stewardship

Global prosperity is inextricably linked to the
health of our planet. Economic reforms must
therefore include commitments to sustainable

development, leveraging green technologies and renewable energy sources to mitigate the impacts of climate change. Investments in sustainable agriculture, water conservation, and pollution control are also critical for ensuring the long-term viability of global economies.

Enhancing Financial Transparency and Regulation

The call for increased transparency and fairness within financial systems can be addressed through reforms aimed at combating corruption, improving regulatory oversight, and enhancing the transparency of financial transactions. Strengthening international cooperation to regulate global finance, combat tax evasion, and prevent money laundering is essential for creating a more equitable economic landscape.

Promoting International Trade and Cooperation

Rather than isolating economies, fostering international trade and cooperation can be a powerful engine for global prosperity. By reducing trade barriers, supporting fair trade practices, and ensuring that trade agreements include provisions for labor rights and environmental protection, nations can create a more balanced and sustainable global trade system.

Investing in Technology and Innovation

The spirit of innovation, often celebrated in the NESARA/GESARA mythology, is indeed a key driver of economic progress. Real-world economic reforms should therefore prioritize investments in research and development, support for startups and small businesses, and education in science, technology, engineering, and mathematics (STEM) fields to spur technological advancements and economic diversification.

Conclusion: A Path Towards Realistic Global Prosperity

While the fantastical elements of NESARA/GESARA may capture the imagination, the path to global prosperity lies in pragmatic, well-considered economic reforms. By focusing on reducing inequality, investing in sustainable development, enhancing financial transparency, and fostering international cooperation, it is possible to work towards a more equitable, stable, and prosperous global economy. The desire for significant economic change is valid and necessary, but achieving such change requires grounded, actionable strategies that address the complexities of the modern world.

Innovation, Ethics, and the Future of Finance

Innovation, Ethics, and the Future of Finance

11.1 Ethical Considerations in Financial Innovation

Balancing Progress with Principles

As the financial sector continues to evolve rapidly, fueled by breakthroughs in technology and shifts in global economic structures, the ethical considerations surrounding these innovations gain paramount importance. This chapter delves into the complex interplay between advancing financial technologies and the ethical frameworks that should guide their development and implementation. It underscores the necessity of aligning financial innovation with ethical standards to ensure that progress benefits society as a whole.

The Ethical Dimensions of Financial Innovation

Financial innovations, from digital currencies and blockchain technology to artificial intelligence (AI) in banking, promise to enhance efficiency, accessibility, and transparency in financial services. However, these advancements also raise critical ethical questions related to privacy, security, equality, and the potential for misuse. Addressing these concerns requires a proactive approach to ethics, one that anticipates potential risks and embeds ethical considerations into the innovation process from the outset.

Privacy and Data Protection

In an age where data is a highly valuable asset, financial innovations leveraging big data analytics and AI pose significant privacy challenges. The ethical handling of personal financial data, consent mechanisms, and data protection measures are central concerns. Ensuring privacy and data protection in financial services not only aligns with ethical norms but also builds trust between consumers and financial institutions.

Inclusivity and Accessibility

Financial innovations have the potential to democratize access to financial services, making banking, lending, and investing more accessible to underserved populations around the world. Ethically, it is imperative to design these innovations in ways that include rather than exclude, bridging the digital divide and preventing the creation of new forms of financial inequality. This entails considering the affordability, usability, and relevance of financial technologies to diverse user groups.

Transparency and Accountability

The complexity of some financial innovations, particularly those involving sophisticated algorithms and opaque blockchain operations, can obscure understanding and hinder accountability. Ethically, there is a duty to ensure that financial products are transparent and that those behind them are accountable for their impacts. This includes clear communication about risks, the mechanisms of new financial instruments, and the responsibilities of different stakeholders in the financial ecosystem.

Preventing Misuse and Ensuring Stability

Financial innovations, while offering numerous benefits, can also be misused for illicit activities, including money laundering, fraud, and financing terrorism. Moreover, the rapid adoption of new financial technologies without adequate oversight can pose risks to financial stability. Ethical financial innovation involves rigorous scrutiny to prevent misuse, alongside mechanisms to identify and mitigate systemic risks early on.

Ethical Frameworks and Regulatory Considerations

Developing ethical frameworks that guide financial innovation requires collaboration between regulators, innovators, ethicists, and consumers. Regulatory bodies play a crucial role in setting standards that ensure innovations are ethically aligned and socially beneficial. However, regulation should also be flexible enough to encourage innovation and adapt to new technologies and market dynamics.

Conclusion: A Principled Path Forward

The future of finance will undoubtedly be shaped by continuous innovation. As we navigate this future, embedding ethical considerations into the heart of financial innovation processes is not just a moral imperative but a strategic necessity. By prioritizing ethics, the financial sector can harness the full potential of emerging technologies to create a more equitable, transparent, and resilient financial system. This principled path forward ensures that financial innovations contribute positively to society, fostering trust and promoting sustainable economic growth.

Sustainable Finance and Social Responsibility

Integrating Sustainability into Financial Decision-Making

The intersection of finance and sustainability has given rise to the concept of sustainable finance, which seeks to incorporate environmental, social, and governance (ESG) criteria into financial services and investment decisions. This chapter explores how sustainable finance and social responsibility are becoming integral to the ethical considerations in the financial sector, driving a shift towards more responsible investment practices and contributing to global efforts to address climate change, social inequalities, and governance issues.

The Rise of ESG Investing

ESG investing represents a major shift in investment strategies, moving beyond traditional financial metrics to include considerations about a company's impact on the environment, its social relationships, and the quality of its governance. Investors are increasingly recognizing that ESG factors can significantly affect a company's performance, risk profile, and long-term sustainability. By integrating ESG criteria, investors aim to generate competitive financial returns while contributing to positive social and environmental outcomes.

Environmental Sustainability: A Financial Imperative

Environmental sustainability has become a critical concern for the financial sector, driven by the growing awareness of climate-related financial risks and the opportunities presented by the transition to a low-carbon economy. Sustainable finance initiatives focus on supporting green technologies, renewable energy projects, and practices that reduce environmental footprints. Green bonds, climate funds, and carbon offsetting instruments are examples of financial products that facilitate investments in environmental sustainability.

Promoting Social Equity Through Finance

Social responsibility in finance encompasses efforts to promote equity, diversity, and inclusion both within the financial industry and through investment practices. This includes providing financial services to underserved communities, supporting projects that create social value, and investing in companies that uphold labor rights and contribute to community development. Social impact investing and microfinance are tools that exemplify how finance can be leveraged to achieve social goals, such as poverty reduction and improved access to education and healthcare.

Governance and Ethical Business Practices

Good governance practices are essential for ensuring that companies operate ethically, transparently, and in the best interests of all stakeholders. Investors are increasingly scrutinizing companies' governance structures, policies on executive pay, anti-corruption measures, and shareholder rights. Sustainable finance advocates for investments in companies that demonstrate strong governance and ethical business practices, recognizing that these factors are indicative of resilience and long-term value creation.

Challenges and Opportunities in Sustainable Finance

While sustainable finance has gained momentum, it faces challenges such as the need for standardized ESG metrics, concerns about greenwashing, and the integration of sustainability into mainstream financial products and services. Addressing these challenges requires collaboration among financial institutions, regulators, investors, and other stakeholders to develop robust frameworks for measuring and reporting on sustainability performance.

Conclusion: Shaping a Sustainable Financial Future

Sustainable finance and social responsibility

represent a paradigm shift in how the financial sector approaches investment and business practices. By prioritizing environmental sustainability, social equity, and responsible governance, the financial industry can play a crucial role in addressing some of the most pressing challenges of our time. As sustainable finance continues to evolve, it offers a path towards a financial system that not only generates economic value but also contributes to a more sustainable and equitable world.

Building the Foundations of Freedom

Building the Foundations of Freedom

12.1 Educating for Financial Literacy and Innovation

Empowering Individuals through Knowledge

In an era marked by rapid economic changes and technological advancements, financial literacy and education in innovation have become critical for individual empowerment and societal progress. This chapter explores the vital role of education in equipping people with the knowledge and skills necessary to navigate the complexities of the modern financial landscape, make informed decisions, and contribute to the innovation economy.

The Importance of Financial Literacy
Financial literacy encompasses understanding fundamental financial concepts such as saving, investing, budgeting, and the responsible use of credit. It is the foundation upon which individuals can build financial stability, plan for the future, and avoid common pitfalls such as excessive debt and financial scams. In the broader sense, financial literacy contributes to the economic health of

society by fostering a populace that participates in financial markets with confidence and competence.

Integrating Financial Education into Curricula

Efforts to enhance financial literacy must begin with the integration of financial education into school curricula. By introducing financial concepts early in education, students can develop a solid understanding of personal finance, the functioning of economies, and the importance of investment and innovation. Practical financial education can help prepare future generations to navigate financial challenges, understand the implications of their financial decisions, and participate effectively in the economy.

Innovation Education for a Changing World

Beyond financial literacy, there is a growing need for education that fosters creativity, critical thinking, and innovation skills. In the context of financial innovation, this includes understanding emerging technologies such as blockchain, artificial intelligence in finance, and the principles of entrepreneurship. Educating for innovation involves encouraging problem-solving, adaptability, and a mindset geared towards continuous learning and improvement.

The Role of Higher Education and Lifelong Learning

Higher education institutions and lifelong learning programs play a crucial role in advancing financial literacy and innovation education. These platforms can offer specialized courses, workshops, and seminars that delve deeper into advanced financial concepts, investment strategies, and the latest innovations in fintech. Moreover, lifelong learning opportunities enable individuals to update their knowledge and skills in response to evolving economic and technological landscapes.

Public and Private Sector Collaboration

Enhancing financial literacy and innovation education requires collaboration between the public and private sectors. Governments, educational institutions, financial organizations, and technology companies can work together to develop educational resources, fund literacy programs, and create initiatives that promote financial inclusion and innovation. Such partnerships can amplify the reach and impact of educational efforts, making financial and innovation literacy accessible to wider audiences.

Conclusion: A Foundation for Prosperous Futures

Educating for financial literacy and innovation is

not just about imparting knowledge; it's about building the foundations for individual empowerment, economic freedom, and societal progress. By equipping individuals with the tools to understand and navigate the financial world, and by fostering a culture of innovation, societies can cultivate resilient economies and unlock the potential for sustainable growth and development. As we look towards the future, the importance of education in financial literacy and innovation remains a pivotal pillar in our collective journey towards prosperity and freedom.

A Call to Action: Patriotism, Innovation, and Financial Freedom

Mobilizing Collective Efforts for a Brighter Future

In the concluding segment of our exploration into the intersections of finance, innovation, and patriotism, we issue a call to action—a unifying appeal to individuals, communities, governments, and institutions to harness the power of innovation and financial literacy for the advancement of societal well-being and the preservation of freedom. This call to action underscores the responsibility of all stakeholders to contribute towards building a future that is grounded in the principles of freedom, innovation, and financial empowerment.

Empowering Individuals with Financial Knowledge

The journey towards financial freedom begins with the individual. It is imperative for people to actively seek knowledge and understanding of financial concepts, tools, and technologies that can enhance their economic well-being. Personal empowerment through financial literacy is a stepping stone towards broader economic freedom and stability, enabling individuals to make informed decisions, manage risks, and capitalize on opportunities.

Fostering Innovation for Economic Prosperity

Innovation is the engine of economic growth and a key driver of competitive advantage in the global economy. Encouraging a culture of creativity, experimentation, and entrepreneurship within communities and industries can spur technological advancements and generate novel solutions to complex challenges. Governments and private sector entities must invest in research and development, support startups and small businesses, and create an environment that nurtures innovation and rewards ingenuity.

Strengthening Communities through Financial Inclusion

Financial freedom and prosperity are not just individual pursuits; they are collective goals that require the active participation and upliftment of entire communities. Promoting financial inclusion by extending access to financial services, education, and resources to underserved and marginalized populations can bridge economic divides and foster a more equitable society. Community-based initiatives, microfinance, and digital financial services are vital tools in this endeavor.

Advocating for Responsible Governance and Policies

Achieving the ideals of freedom, innovation, and financial prosperity necessitates governance and policies that reflect these values. Advocacy for transparent, accountable, and responsive governance is crucial. Policymakers must be guided by the principles of economic freedom, enacting regulations that stimulate innovation, protect consumer rights, and ensure fair and open markets. Public dialogue and participation in the policymaking process are essential for crafting policies that are in the best interest of society.

Collaborating for a Sustainable and Prosperous Future

The challenges and opportunities of the 21st

century demand a collaborative approach. By working together, governments, businesses, non-profits, and citizens can leverage their collective strengths to drive progress towards a sustainable and prosperous future. This includes partnerships that advance sustainable development goals, initiatives that promote global financial stability, and collaborations that harness the transformative power of technology for good.

Conclusion: Heeding the Call

The call to action for patriotism, innovation, and financial freedom is an invitation to each of us to play an active role in shaping the future. It is a reminder that the foundations of freedom are built on the collective efforts of individuals and societies who are committed to the ideals of liberty, equality, and prosperity. By embracing financial literacy, fostering innovation, and working towards an inclusive and equitable economic system, we can ensure that the foundations of our democracy remain strong for generations to come. Together, let us heed this call and commit to building a future that honors our shared values and aspirations.

Embrace the Future:

Unlock Your Financial Potential with Cryptocurrency

A New Era of Opportunity Awaits

The digital age has ushered in transformative changes, reshaping the way we think about finance, investment, and economic empowerment. At the forefront of this revolution is cryptocurrency—a medium that not only symbolizes innovation and progress but also presents a unique opportunity for individuals around the globe to participate in the financial markets. As we navigate through the realms of inclusion, leveraging new technology, and enhancing financial prosperity for all, we invite you to explore the dynamic world of cryptocurrency and consider opening a trading account to make informed, reasonable investments.

Democratizing Finance

Cryptocurrency stands as a beacon of financial democratization, offering access to investment opportunities that were once out of reach for many. Whether you're an experienced investor or

116

new to the financial markets, the world of cryptocurrency provides an accessible platform for you to engage with and benefit from. By embracing this digital currency, you're not just participating in an economic trend; you're joining a global movement towards financial inclusion and empowerment.

Leveraging Technology for Growth

The technology behind cryptocurrency—blockchain—is renowned for its security, transparency, and efficiency. These attributes make cryptocurrency an appealing option for those looking to diversify their investment portfolios. Investing in cryptocurrency allows you to leverage cutting-edge technology for personal financial growth, aligning your assets with the future of finance.

A Path to Financial Prosperity

The journey into cryptocurrency trading is one of potential and promise. While the market is known for its volatility, it also offers the possibility of significant returns. Educated and reasonable investments in cryptocurrency can be a valuable component of a diversified investment strategy, contributing to your overall financial prosperity.

An Invitation to Explore

We understand that the world of cryptocurrency may seem complex and daunting at first glance. That's why we encourage you to approach this opportunity with curiosity and caution. To assist you on this journey, we will provide a reference section with links to reputable sources where you can research the pros and cons of cryptocurrency investment. This knowledge will empower you to make informed decisions that best suit your financial goals and risk tolerance.

Embracing the Future Together

As we stand on the brink of a new financial frontier, the possibilities are endless. Opening a cryptocurrency trading account is more than a financial decision; it's a step towards embracing innovation, exploring new opportunities, and participating in the economic evolution. Let us embrace the future of finance together, unlocking the door to financial opportunities that await.

Join Us

Dive into the world of cryptocurrency and discover the potential it holds for enhancing your financial future. By taking advantage of this emerging market, you're not just investing in digital currency; you're investing in your potential for growth, innovation, and prosperity. Welcome to the future of finance—your journey begins now.

Introduction to Uphold

Uphold represents a comprehensive digital finance platform that empowers users to seamlessly engage in transactions with a variety of assets, including a broad spectrum of cryptocurrencies and traditional currencies such as the USD and EUR. It stands out by simplifying the processes of buying, selling, holding, trading, exchanging, and transferring funds across different asset types. With a mission to democratize access to financial services globally, Uphold combines a straightforward user interface with competitive pricing structures to enhance affordability and accessibility of financial operations for a diverse user base.

Enhanced Features of Uphold:

- Diverse Asset Portfolio: Uphold sets itself apart with its robust support for multiple assets. This includes leading cryptocurrencies like Bitcoin (BTC), Ethereum (ETH), and Ripple (XRP), alongside key fiat currencies such as the US Dollar (USD), Euro (EUR), and British Pound (GBP), catering to a wide range of investment preferences and needs.

- Real-Time Transactions: The platform distinguishes itself with the capability for instant transactions, enabling users to promptly buy, sell, or swap assets without experiencing the delays often encountered in traditional financial setups.

- Competitive Pricing Model: By offering transaction fees that are notably lower than those typically found in conventional banking systems, Uphold prioritizes affordability in financial transactions.

- User-Centric Design: Aimed at both cryptocurrency enthusiasts and those exploring diversification of their investment portfolio, Uphold's platform is intuitively designed for ease of use, ensuring accessibility for users with varying levels of experience in digital finance.

- Stringent Security Protocols: Uphold prioritizes the security of its users' assets and personal data through the implementation of advanced security strategies. This includes rigorous encryption standards, the deployment of two-factor authentication (2FA) for additional account protection, and the strategic use of cold storage solutions to safeguard cryptocurrency holdings.

- Regulatory Adherence and User Protection: Operating under strict regulatory oversight in the United States, Uphold adheres to comprehensive financial regulations. This commitment to compliance underpins the platform's dedication to ensuring the security and integrity of user funds and transactions.

Uphold emerges as a forward-thinking solution for individuals and investors seeking a versatile and secure platform for managing a diverse array of digital and traditional assets. Through its user-friendly design, competitive fee structure, and a strong emphasis on security and regulatory compliance, Uphold is crafting a more inclusive financial ecosystem that aligns with the evolving demands and expectations of the global market. Discover Uphold, where simplicity meets efficiency in trading. Consider creating your account to explore a trading experience designed for ease and cost-effectiveness.

https://bit.ly/TradeCoinApp

Introducing CoinMarketCap

Launched in 2013 by Brandon Chez, CoinMarketCap has rapidly ascended to become the premier destination for timely, comprehensive insights into the cryptocurrency market. This platform stands out as a critical resource for both newcomers and seasoned investors in the cryptocurrency space, offering a vast array of data on market capitalizations, price fluctuations, trading volumes, and essential details pertaining to a wide range of cryptocurrencies.

Expansive Cryptocurrency Listings

CoinMarketCap distinguishes itself by cataloging an extensive selection of cryptocurrencies. From the giants of the industry like Bitcoin and Ethereum to the emerging altcoins making waves in the market, the platform ensures users have access to a wealth of detailed information. This includes real-time updates on prices, market capitalizations, trading volumes, circulating supplies, and historical performance, among other critical metrics.

In-Depth Market Data

The site excels in delivering real-time, across-the-board data on cryptocurrency prices as observed on multiple exchanges. This feature is invaluable for users aiming to execute informed trading decisions by comparing prices, trading volumes, and market movements across a variety of trading platforms.

Comprehensive Portfolio Tracking

CoinMarketCap's portfolio tracking functionality offers users a streamlined way to oversee their cryptocurrency investments. By aggregating their holdings in one intuitive interface, investors can monitor their portfolio's value, performance, and trends over time, simplifying the management of their digital assets.

Curated News and Expert Analysis

Understanding the need for reliable information in the fast-paced crypto environment, CoinMarketCap provides a curated selection of news articles, in-depth analyses, and insightful commentary. This ensures users are well-informed about the latest market trends, technological advancements, regulatory updates, and significant events shaping the cryptocurrency landscape.

Robust Tools and Educational Resources

Beyond market data, CoinMarketCap is a treasure

trove of tools and resources designed to enrich the user's understanding and navigation of the cryptocurrency market. Historical price charts, market heatmaps, exchange rankings, and educational guides are just a few examples of the resources available. These tools are designed to empower users with the knowledge and insights needed to navigate the cryptocurrency market confidently.

API Services for Developers

Recognizing the diverse needs of the cryptocurrency community, CoinMarketCap also offers comprehensive API services. These services enable developers to seamlessly integrate cryptocurrency market data into applications, websites, and other platforms, facilitating access to accurate and real-time information.

A Gateway to Cryptocurrency Mastery

CoinMarketCap has solidified its status as an indispensable platform for anyone engaged with the cryptocurrency market. Whether you're taking your first steps into the world of digital currencies or you're an experienced trader seeking granular data and analysis, CoinMarketCap provides the tools, information, and insights necessary to stay ahead in the dynamic and evolving cryptocurrency ecosystem.

Websites where people can learn about potential investments in cryptocurrency:

- CoinMarketCap: CoinMarketCap is a website that offers real-time information on cryptocurrency prices, market capitalization, trading volume, and historical data. It can be a valuable resource for individuals researching potential investments in the cryptocurrency market.

- Investopedia: Investopedia is a well-known financial education website that covers a wide range of topics, including cryptocurrencies. It offers articles, tutorials, and guides to help individuals understand the basics of investing in cryptocurrencies and make informed decisions.

- CryptoSlate: CryptoSlate is a cryptocurrency news and information platform that provides insights into various cryptocurrencies, blockchain projects, and market trends. It can be a useful resource for staying updated on potential investment opportunities in the crypto space.

- Binance Academy: Binance Academy is an educational platform created by the popular cryptocurrency exchange Binance. It offers courses, articles, and videos on blockchain technology, cryptocurrencies, and trading strategies to help users navigate the world of digital assets.

Crypto Learning Resources

There are numerous books that offer insightful perspectives into the world of cryptocurrency, ranging from introductory guides for beginners to in-depth analyses for seasoned investors. Here's a selection of notable books that cover various aspects of cryptocurrency:

Cryptocurrency books on Amazon:

https://amzn.to/42BOBeM

1. **"The Bitcoin Standard: The Decentralized Alternative to Central Banking" by Saifedean Ammous** - This book delves into the economic properties that have allowed Bitcoin to grow quickly and explores its potential impact on the global financial system.

2. **"Mastering Bitcoin: Unlocking Digital Cryptocurrencies" by Andreas M. Antonopoulos** - Aimed at developers and technical enthusiasts, this book provides a comprehensive guide to understanding Bitcoin at a technical level.

3. **"Digital Gold: Bitcoin and the Inside Story of the Misfits and Millionaires Trying to Reinvent

Money" by Nathaniel Popper** - "Digital Gold" tells the fascinating story of the rise of Bitcoin, introducing readers to its creators and early adopters who have shaped the cryptocurrency world.

4. **"Cryptoassets: The Innovative Investor's Guide to Bitcoin and Beyond" by Chris Burniske and Jack Tatar** - This book offers a detailed analysis of how to value bitcoin and other cryptoassets, providing a framework for investing in this new asset class.

5. **"Blockchain Basics: A Non-Technical Introduction in 25 Steps" by Daniel Drescher** - Perfect for readers who are new to blockchain technology, this book breaks down blockchain into easy-to-understand concepts without delving into complex technical details.

6. **"The Age of Cryptocurrency: How Bitcoin and Digital Money Are Challenging the Global Economic Order" by Paul Vigna and Michael J. Casey** - This book explores how cryptocurrency can go beyond being a simple digital currency and create a new financial paradigm.

7. **"Cryptocurrency: How Bitcoin and Digital Money are Challenging the Global Economic Order" by Paul Vigna and Michael J. Casey** - Similar in title to their other work but focusing

more on the broader implications of cryptocurrency, this book examines the potential for digital currencies to change the world.

8. **"The Truth Machine: The Blockchain and the Future of Everything" by Paul Vigna and Michael J. Casey** - Another insightful book from Vigna and Casey, this one focuses on how blockchain technology could revolutionize various sectors beyond finance.

9. **"Bitcoin Billionaires: A True Story of Genius, Betrayal, and Redemption" by Ben Mezrich** - This narrative follows the fascinating journey of the Winklevoss twins as they become among the first bitcoin billionaires.

10. **"The Internet of Money" by Andreas M. Antonopoulos** - Spread across three volumes, these books explore the philosophical and social implications of bitcoin and blockchain technology, making the case for why the world needs bitcoin.

Each of these books provides a unique perspective on cryptocurrency and blockchain, catering to a wide range of interests from the technical to the economic, and even the social impact of this digital revolution.

Web-Based Crypto Training Programs

1. <u>Coursera:</u> Coursera offers various online courses related to cryptocurrency and blockchain technology. Some popular courses include "Bitcoin and Cryptocurrency Technologies" by Princeton University and "Blockchain Basics" by the University at Buffalo. These courses provide a comprehensive understanding of the fundamentals of cryptocurrencies, blockchain technology, and their applications.

2. Udemy: Udemy is another platform that offers a wide range of crypto training programs for beginners to advanced users. Courses like "Cryptocurrency Investment Course 2021: Fund Your Retirement!" and "Blockchain and Cryptocurrency Explained" are designed to educate individuals on how to navigate the world of cryptocurrencies effectively.

https://amzn.to/4bCtBsv

In the "QFS, Nesara/Gesara, and 2060" series, you'll discover the keys to navigating the dynamic landscape of finance in the digital age. Dive into the world of cryptocurrencies, decentralized finance (DeFi), and blockchain technology as you uncover the potential of these groundbreaking innovations to revolutionize the way we interact with money, invest in assets, and conduct transactions.

In this comprehensive series, you'll explore the intricacies of cryptocurrencies such as Bitcoin, Ethereum, and Ripple (XRP), learning about their underlying technology, market dynamics, and investment opportunities. Gain insights into the principles of decentralized finance and explore the diverse ecosystem of DeFi platforms, protocols, and applications reshaping traditional financial services.

But the journey doesn't stop there. The

"Cryptocurrency Unlocked" series also delves into broader topics shaping the future of finance, including the NESARA (National Economic Security and Recovery Act) and GESARA (Global Economic Security and Reformation Act) initiatives, which propose radical reforms to the global financial system. Discover the potential implications of these ambitious plans and how they could reshape the economic landscape in the years to come.

Furthermore, the series explores the cutting-edge Quantum Financial System (QFS), a revolutionary paradigm that leverages quantum computing and blockchain technology to create a more secure, transparent, and efficient financial infrastructure. Learn about the principles behind the QFS and its potential to transform the way we transact, invest, and store value in the digital era.

Finally, journey into the future with the book "2060," a speculative exploration of the potential consequences of emerging technologies, societal trends, and geopolitical shifts on the world of finance. From AI-powered trading algorithms to digital currencies issued by central banks, "2060" offers a glimpse into a future where finance is more interconnected, automated, and decentralized than ever before.

Join us as we unlock the secrets of the new world of finance in the "QFS, Nesara/Gesara, and 2060" series. Whether you're a seasoned investor, a curious newcomer, or simply intrigued by the possibilities of the digital revolution, this series will empower you to navigate the complex landscape of finance in the 21st century and beyond.

Bruce Goldwell's

Web Site

Www.MyKindleBooks.net

About The Author

Bruce Goldwell is a self-help/motivational author and creator of two captivating fantasy adventures, "Dragon Keepers" a six book series and "Starfighters Defending Earth" a three book series. He is an inspiring figure who has overcome significant challenges in his life. As a Vietnam veteran, he experienced homelessness for over ten years. During these difficult times, Bruce developed a compassionate heart and strong desire to uplift others. While living on the streets, he immersed himself in motivational literature at local bookstores, where he found solace in the works of renowned authors such as the creators of Chicken Soup for the Soul, Bob Proctor, and David Stanley, Elvis Presley's brother.

Inspired by the transformative impact of the film "The Secret," Goldwell penned his first book, "Mastery of Abundant Living: The Keys to Mastering the Law of

Attraction." He had the honor of personally presenting the first autographed copy to Bob Proctor. Recognizing that young readers may not typically engage with self-help material, Goldwell brilliantly crafted a fantastical adventure series for teens. Within these enchanting stories, he weaves principles of success and powerful life lessons to ignite hope and encourage personal growth in younger audiences.

Driven by an unwavering belief in the power of his books to change lives, Bruce Goldwell's moving journey from homeless veteran to impactful author has resonated with thousands around the globe. His triumphant quest to help others is a testament to resilience, determination, and the transformative power of words.

Www.mykindlebooks.net